ABIDE with ME

Prayers for Life's Eventide

CARLEE HALLMAN

DIMENSIONS
FOR LIVING
NASHVILLE

ABIDE WITH ME
PRAYERS FOR LIFE'S EVENTIDE

Library of Congress Cataloging-in-Publication Data

Hallman, Carlee L. 1929-
    Abide with me : prayers for life's eventide / Carlee L. Hallman.
        p. cm.
    Includes bibliographical references.
    ISBN 0-687-49220-3 (binding: pbk., adhesive : alk. paper)
    1. Older people—Prayer-books and devotions—English. I. Title.
    BV4580.H23 2006
    242'.85—dc22

                                                                      2006016023

Interior photos: DigitalVision and Creatas.

06 07 08 09 10 11 12 13 14 15—10 9 8 7 6 5 4 3 2 1
MANUFACTURED IN THE UNITED STATES OF AMERICA

Dedicated to my husband, Howard,
who made this possible

Contents

CONTENTS

LAMENT

CONFESSION

CONTENTS

THANK YOU

CONTENTS

PRESENCE

CONTENTS

Introduction

As I wrote this book of prayers for the later years, I realized that older people have been a source of love, encouragement, and inspiration throughout my life. It began with my grandparents. During my seminary training, my internship was at a nursing home as a chaplain. The support and kindness of the residents was heartening as I began this second career. Throughout my ministry in small churches, I was inspired by the faith and lives of the older people. Since retiring, I continue to conduct a monthly worship service at a nursing home. But nothing prepares one for aging like aging itself.

From my experience of visiting with seniors in homes, retirement centers, and nursing homes, I have found prayer to be a great resource for them. A book of prayers that points the way to faith in the varying circumstances of aging can give voice to our deep concerns. It can also be helpful in raising sensitive issues, which then can be shared and discussed.

These prayers are written in the first-person voice, whether they reflect my own experiences or are written with someone else in mind. Some readers may recognize themselves as they read the prayers and realize that the experience of faith expressed may inspire someone else. Each prayer is accompanied by a Bible verse that gives context to our faith and adds further dimension. In addition, the prayers appear in large-print text to make them easier to read.

As we share the joys, sorrows, vexations, praise, and thanksgiving in prayer, we realize that we are not alone. God is our companion, and we are surrounded by a "great cloud of witnesses." Prayer opens the door.

TRUST

"Truly I tell you, whoever does not receive the kingdom of God as a little child will never enter it."

—*Mark 10:15*

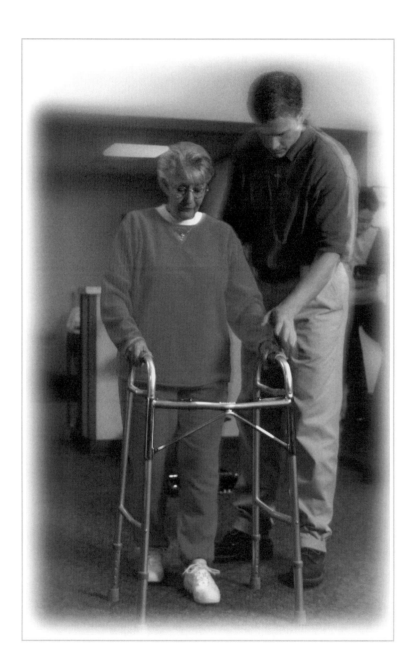

An Adventure

Lord, every day
of growing older
is an adventure:
how to make the bed
when arthritis buzzes,
how to go upstairs
after a knee replacement,
how to eat properly
with a tooth removed.
You expect us to keep going.
My friends and I
share our little tricks
for getting around barriers.
Do we tickle you, Lord,
with our creativity?
Your Spirit is never contained.
We follow you,
even when we don't know
what will happen next.

John 3:8:
**"The wind blows where it chooses, and you hear the
sound of it, but you do not know where it comes from
or where it goes. So it is with everyone who is born of
the Spirit."**

I Can't Wait

Waiting is hard work, Lord.
Waiting for a call from the doctor,
for a letter from a loved one,
for my ride to arrive,
for answers to prayer.
While I wait, Lord,
I work the crossword puzzle,
accomplish five-minute tasks
that have been put off,
pace anxiously.
Calm me down, Lord.
Give me patience.
Assure me that
all is well and
all will be well.

Psalm 37:7a:
Be still before the LORD, and wait patiently for him.

Psalm 40:1:
I waited patiently for the LORD;
**   he inclined to me and heard my cry.**

What If's

As I look back over my life, Father,
I ask myself,
"What if I had gone that way?
What if I had done that?"
If I could live several lives
and compare them,
maybe I would get it right.
You give us only one life
and guide us with your Spirit.
You expect us to walk by faith,
not by sight.
I haven't always done that.
I wish I had.
Help me to rely on your care
and go forward.

2 Corinthians 5:6-7:
So we are always confident; even though we know that
while we are at home in the body we are away from
the Lord—for we walk by faith, not by sight.

In Your Care

O Lord, I have been
diagnosed with Alzheimer's.
I see in others
what lies ahead.
I am in assisted living now,
but for how long?
Yesterday I looked at my clock,
but I couldn't remember
what it meant.
I don't know when
to go for meals.
My neighbor tries to help.
Today I was stuck
in the elevator
and didn't know what to do
until someone else got on
and let me out.
I am your child, Lord.
Hold my hand
so I am not afraid.

1 Peter 5:7:
Cast all your anxiety on him, because he cares for you.

Hold Me, Lord

Lord, I look out of this body.
I cannot speak.
I can move one hand
and blink.
People ask me things.
I cannot answer.

I used to be so independent.
Now, all I can do is wait
for someone to turn
the TV on and off.
I get moved out of bed
to a wheelchair and back
whether I will or not.
Some hands are gentle,
some are rough.

I rely on your hands, O Lord,
to lift me up and
keep my spirit safe.

Psalm 4:8:
I will both lie down and sleep in peace;
    for you alone, O LORD, make me lie down in safety.

Routine

Some days I get out of bed
and look forward to my routine:
coffee, crossword puzzle,
making the bed,
watering the plants,
and time with you.
It is comforting to have structure.
Other days,
routine keeps me from
the surprise of discovery
and is burdensome.
Whether I am being creative
or efficient,
you are my source
and inspiration, Lord.
You give life.

John 10:10b:
"I came that they may have life, and have it abundantly."

Troubled

The waters are troubled, Lord.
I can feel it,
in our family,
in our nation,
in the world.
In an earlier time
I would have plunged in,
tried to find the cause,
and done something about it.
Now my strength is gone.
I wait to see what will happen.
If I did not know
you are in charge, Lord,
I would be afraid.

Psalm 46:1-2a:
God is our refuge and strength,
** a very present help in trouble.**
Therefore we will not fear.

Hymn: "This Is My Father's World"

Why?

When I see wispy clouds
against blue sky
and breezes sifting snow
through pine branches,
I am filled with joy
that such beauty exists
for all to enjoy.
Then I wonder why
there is such evil
that our world is threatened
with nuclear destruction.
How do I interpret
your forbearance, God?
Yet will I trust
that you will bring
all to fruition
in your time, O God of Creation.

Psalm 146:3, 5-6a:
Do not put your trust in princes,
   in mortals, in whom there is no help . . .
Happy are those whose help is the God of Jacob,
   whose hope is in the LORD their God,
who made heaven and earth.

Rainbows

O Creator God,
as I stand sprinkling
the garden with the hose,
I see rainbows.
When I was a child
and afraid of many things,
my mother showed me a rainbow
and told of your promise.
It made me feel safe.
I wonder if the children today
know that you still rule the world.
They need you more than ever.
O Creator God,
help me to share my faith
so others
may find strength.

Genesis 9:15-16a:
**I will remember my covenant that is between me and
you and every living creature of all flesh; and the
waters shall never again become a flood to destroy all
flesh. When the bow is in the clouds, I will see it and
remember.**

Diets

My husband brought
a bunch of roses
and doughnuts
from the grocery
this morning.
Yesterday I made
cookies
and a mince pie.
We are bad
for each other's diets,
but it's hard to watch
our cholesterol
all the time.
We rely on love
to fill in the rest.
Your love, O Lord, is
the essential ingredient.

1 John 4:7:
**Beloved, let us love one another, because love is from
God; everyone who loves is born of God and knows
God.**

1 Corinthians 10:23:
**"All things are lawful," but not all things are benefi-
cial. "All things are lawful," but not all things build up.**

ASKING

"Ask, and it will be given you; search, and you will find; knock, and the door will be opened for you."

—*Matthew 7:7*

Inspiration

O Holy Spirit,
you give myriad reminders
of your love:
this misty morning
of chirping birds,
the touch of
a loved one,
words of forgiveness,
and the heart
stretching to include
diverse others.
Thank you, Spirit of Love.
Smooth and soften my
heart's hard edges,
that I may live love
like a stream
flowing with life-giving water.

John 7:38b-39a:
**"As the scripture has said, 'Out of the believer's heart
shall flow rivers of living water.'" Now he said this
about the Spirit.**

Communication

Are people talking faster
or is my mind slowing down?
People on TV
speak so quickly
I lose half of it,
even with closed captioning.
Someone told me
that computer games
would speed up my reflexes.
When your people were slow
to understand, Holy God,
you sent Jesus
as the Word made flesh
to communicate your way.
Let me be quick to grasp
what is important
for your kingdom, Holy God.
Show me, even if I am slow.

John 1:14:
**And the Word became flesh and lived among us, and
we have seen his glory, the glory as of a father's only
son, full of grace and truth.**

Show Us Your Way

Lord Jesus, five years ago
my friend and I began
going to church together.
Now my friend is on a walker,
and I am none too steady.
We can barely get to church
and home again.
People tell us to ask
for a ride.
We could do that once.
But 365 times is too much.
There are options: taxis,
television, Bible reading
to consider.
Guide our ways, Lord.
We need your care.

Psalm 31:3:
You are indeed my rock and my fortress;
     for your name's sake lead me and guide me.

Our Daily Bread

Lord, you taught us
to pray for our daily bread
and not to be led into temptation.
Now trays of food are set before me;
and if I ate it all,
the nurses would no longer
be able to lift me.
When I was active,
I could eat more;
but even then extra weight
was hard on my knees.
Help me, Lord.
I remember your answer
in the wilderness
when the temptation was bread.
Strengthen me
so I do not yield
to overeating.

Matthew 4:4:
But he answered, "It is written, 'One does not live by bread alone, but by every word that comes from the mouth of God.'"

Living Praise

The maidenhair fern
shivers with the slightest breeze,
while the stiff holly leaves stand firm.
O Creative God,
your many plants
complement one another.
When your people
live their lives in praise of you,
differences add to the harmony
and enjoyment.
Help us to grow in integrity
and in respect for others,
O God of the Universe,
that we may glorify you on earth.

Psalm 133:1:
How very good and pleasant it is
when kindred live together in unity!

Opening Jars

Gracious Lord,
my hands hurt.
It's hard to open jars
and plastic packages,
to weed my garden,
or even to hold a book.
These hands
have given years of good service;
but, Lord, what am I going to do
in the end to be useful?
Aspirin is not the answer.
Help me see
new possibilities,
new ways of being.

Luke 10:41:
But the Lord answered her, "Martha, Martha, you are worried and distracted by many things; there is need of only one thing. Mary has chosen the better part, which will not be taken away from her."

Hymn: "Take My Life, and Let It Be"

Move Me

It is Easter,
and I stand in silent awe
before the empty tomb.
And then, surprised,
I realize
that the disciples
were not energized
by seeing you alive.
No! It was later
when your Holy Spirit came
that they were galvanized,
from hiding in the upper room,
into action.
Fill me, O Lord,
with your Spirit
that, moved from lethargy,
I bring your healing message to others.

Acts 2:2-4:
**And suddenly from heaven there came a sound like
the rush of a violent wind, and it filled the entire
house where they were sitting. Divided tongues, as of
fire, appeared among them, and a tongue rested on**

each of them. All of them were filled with the Holy Spirit and began to speak in other languages, as the Spirit gave them ability.

Hymn: "Breathe on Me, Breath of God"

Pentecost

O Spirit of the Living God,
we celebrate your coming
at Pentecost.
Fall on us
that we may live abundantly.
Empower us
that your kingdom
will come on earth
and others may share
in the joy
of peace,
and the wholeness
and excitement
of being fully alive.
Come!

Acts 2:38:
Peter said to them, "Repent, and be baptized every
one of you in the name of Jesus Christ so that your
sins may be forgiven; and you will receive the gift of
the Holy Spirit."

I Need Help

Lord, you want us to value each person,
but it's not easy
when the other person
whistles or drums with her fingers all day.
You want us to leave judgment to you.
Help me to look
for the spark of your presence
in the other person
and fan it to life.
Help me to love
when reason fails.
Remind me to be humble, Lord,
and keep friendship open.

John 13:34-35:
"I give you a new commandment, that you love one another. Just as I have loved you, you also should love one another. By this everyone will know that you are my disciples, if you have love for one another."

John 14:15-17a:
"If you love me, you will keep my commandments. And I will ask the Father, and he will give you another Advocate, to be with you forever. This is the Spirit of truth."

Under a Bushel Basket

Lord, yesterday I went to visit
as your servant, and yet,
I didn't speak of you directly.
Were you guiding me,
or did I miss my cue?
I don't want to hide
your light under a bushel.
Have I buried your pearl
under layers of fear
of being pushy
or inappropriate?
Help me, Lord,
to speak your word
to those in need,
that we may fully
share your presence.

Matthew 5:15-16:
**"No one after lighting a lamp puts it under the bushel
basket, but on the lampstand, and it gives light to all
in the house. In the same way, let your light shine
before others, so that they may see your good works
and give glory to your Father in heaven."**

Looking Ahead

O Great Creator God,
when the sun
glistens on pine needles
and the furry spider
dangles from its web,
I marvel
at the splendor
of your creation
of which we are part.
Take away my anxiety
about the natural order
that ends in physical decline;
rather, give me faith
in that which is to come.

2 Corinthians 5:1:
For we know that if the earthly tent we live in is destroyed, we have a building from God, a house not made with hands, eternal in the heavens.

Remind Me

When rain streaks down
from leaden skies
and I feel gloomy,
remind me, Lord,
to give thanks
that I am warm and dry.
I remember camping trips
when I was younger,
with rain dripping
into the tent
and cold creeping
into my veins.
Now every night
I have a warm, soft bed;
dry clothing;
no mosquitoes.
How often you give blessings
we take for granted.
Remind me to be thankful, Lord.

Psalm 136:26:
O give thanks to the God of heaven,
for his steadfast love endures forever.

I Need Butter

Now that I'm ninety-five, Lord,
I reach for the pats of butter.
At this age,
this little indulgence
isn't going to kill me.

There is so much that is grim
and sordid in the news.
We have to have a little joy.

I gave up coffee for green tea
years ago. But butter—
let's face it,
if I had a
heart attack today,
they'd say I died of old age.

Keep me in humor, Lord,
as I wait to see you face-to-face.

1 Corinthians 13:12:
For now we see in a mirror, dimly, but then we will see
face to face. Now I know only in part; then I will know
fully, even as I have been fully known.

War-Torn

Dear Lord, bamboo shoots
come up like rockets
in the midst of my flowers.
They are grim reminders of war,
with the flowers as the
innocent bystanders.
Dear Lord, give strength
and hope to those
whose lives and families
are torn apart
by forces that they
cannot control.
Have mercy, Lord,
on us all.

Psalm 62:1-2:
For God alone my soul waits in silence;
    from him comes my salvation.
He alone is my rock and my salvation,
    my fortress; I shall never be shaken.

Psalm 62:8:
Trust in him at all times, O people;
    pour out your heart before him;
    God is a refuge for us.

Ice Storm

Ice covers the trees
and sparkles on the walks.
The streets are treacherous.
I am thankful
that I can stay in
and keep warm.
Being retired has its rewards.
It's not a good day
for the mailman
or for drivers.
Keep them safe, Lord.
The ice reminds me
of times I might have slipped.
Your care
in time of need
keeps us
upright on our way.

Psalm 94:18:
When I thought, "My foot is slipping,"
    your steadfast love, O LORD, held me up.

Psalm 18:36:
You gave me a wide place for my steps under me,
    and my feet did not slip.

Accidents

Sirens go by.
Someone is in trouble, Lord.
When I landed in the street
after my car crash,
I raised my head
and asked, "What happened?"
A woman said,
"You have been in an accident."
Then she picked up something
and wrapped my fingers around it.
I found it there later
in the hospital.
It was a button from my coat.
What a kind thing to do!
I pray, O Lord,
that those in accidents today
may know your love
is with them yet.

Psalm 139:7-8:
Where can I go from your spirit?
  Or where can I flee from your presence?
If I ascend to heaven, you are there;
  if I make my bed in Sheol, you are there.

Spirit

How quickly the flower fades.
O Lord God, the older I get,
the shorter the time on earth seems.
Yet, as sunlight
shines through flower petals,
I am reminded of those
in my life
who seemed to shine
with light from within.
They have been like beacons
showing me the way.
Many of them were older.
Fill me with your Spirit, Lord,
that as I weaken,
your presence within
becomes stronger
that I may yet light the way
for others.

Luke 11:13b:
**". . . how much more will the heavenly Father give the
Holy Spirit to those who ask him!"**

Isaiah 40:8:
The grass withers, the flower fades;
but the word of our God will stand forever.

A New Day

O Lord of Creation,
this morning
the windows are frosted.
Delicate patterns
sparkle in the sun:
a reminder
of all that's fresh and beautiful.
Help me to let go
of yesterday's
turmoil and sorrow.
Forgive us all.
Make me new
this morning,
recreated
in your image.

Philippians 3:13b-14:
Forgetting what lies behind and straining forward to what lies ahead, I press on toward the goal for the prize of the heavenly call of God in Christ Jesus.

Be My Valentine

It's Valentine's Day.
My sweetheart is gone.
We never had children,
but I have dear nieces
and nephews.
Will they think of me?
O Spirit of love,
don't let me moan and groan,
rather let me bask
in memories of love.
Open my heart
that I may show love
for someone
who needs it today.

1 John 4:19:
We love because he first loved us.

1 John 4:16b:
God is love, and those who abide in love abide in God, and God abides in them.

Seasonal Dysfunction

Lord of All, summer is over;
and fall, with its
descending bits and pieces,
reminds me of my crumbling
physical defenses,
as winter looms ahead.
Yet in the somber brown
and white season,
there is the red and green
of Christmas
and the red
of Valentine's Day,
which remind us of your love.
Keep me growing
and green in your Spirit
no matter what the season.

Romans 8:6:
To set the mind on the flesh is death, but to set the mind on the Spirit is life and peace.

Thirsty

How straight and tall
the tulips stood
yesterday,
when they had water.
Now they flop,
leaves and flowers askew.
I wish I'd watered them.
I too sometimes droop, Lord.
Fill me with your living water
that I may stand tall
and be filled with
inner vitality
in my old age.

John 4:13-14:
Jesus said to her, "Everyone who drinks of this water will be thirsty again, but those who drink of the water that I will give them will never be thirsty. The water that I will give will become in them a spring of water gushing up to eternal life."

Conversation

O Lord, my friend talks so much
I can't get a word in edgewise.
It's hard for me to listen
when I can't respond.
My mind wanders.
Should I say something to her?
What if she's offended?
Lord, is that what we sound like to you
when we ask and ask
and don't wait for answers?
Help me listen
to you and to my friend
with my heart,
then it will work out.
Thank you for listening.

Matthew 18:15b:
"Go and point out the fault when the two of you are alone. If the member listens to you, you have regained that one."

Retirement

O Lord, retirement
is not so easy.
I wake up raring to go
and don't know
what to do.
I reorganized
my wife's cupboards,
and she was not pleased.
Good causes always
need volunteers,
but it's not the same as
a paid job.
Help me, Lord,
to be open to new ways to serve
that will both challenge
and fulfill.

Romans 12:11:
Do not lag in zeal, be ardent in spirit, serve the Lord.

Psalm 92:14:
In old age they [the righteous] still produce fruit;
they are always green and full of sap.

Psalm 25:9:
He leads the humble in what is right,
and teaches the humble his way.

Change in the Air

How fascinated we are
by things that float
in the air:
leaves, snow, oobleck, confetti.
Snow globes catch the idea.
Today leaves let go
and fall straight down.
It seems a celebration of change.
Now I must move
and let go of many things.
They tell me
that I am unreliable.
As I step into the unknown,
Lord, hold me up.
Strengthen my faith.
Help me enjoy
this new adventure.

Mark 9:23-24:
Jesus said to him, "If you are able!—All things can be done for the one who believes." Immediately the father of the child cried out, "I believe; help my unbelief!"

Hymn: "Leaning on the Everlasting Arms"

Drowsy

O Merciful God,
the speaker is droning on and on.
He talks fast.
I can barely hear him,
even though he has a microphone.
After a heavy lunch
it is hard to stay awake.
At our table people are nodding off.
I don't want to jerk suddenly
and give myself away.
Have mercy, O Lord.
We need help.

Acts 20:9:
A young man named Eutychus, who was sitting in the window, began to sink off into a deep sleep while Paul talked still longer.

LAMENT

Then they cried to the LORD in their trouble,
and he brought them out from their distress.

—*Psalm 107:28*

A Cry!

O Lord, you know
my precious one
is fading
week by week.
I hold his hand,
talk, remember.
Sometimes he smiles,
squeezes my hand.
Sometimes tears flow.
Lord, it's my life too,
ebbing away.
Help me to bear up,
find deeper meaning.
You are my hope
of eternal love.
Don't let me down.
I need
your love beyond all loves
now.

Psalm 23:4a (KJV):
**Yea, though I walk through the valley of the shadow
of death, I will fear no evil: for thou art with me.**

In the Pits

I'm in the pits, Lord.
Like Jeremiah (in Jeremiah 38:6)
I'm up to my neck in mire.
Mine is not physical,
but of the spirit,
dark and despondent.
I can't move.
Pull me up, Lord,
don't let go.
I bow my head
before you
and rest.
You are my Creator,
O God;
save me.
In You, I put my trust.

Psalm 40:1-2:
I waited patiently for the LORD;
he inclined to me and heard my cry.
He drew me up from the desolate pit,
out of the miry bog,
and set my feet upon a rock,
making my steps secure.

Need Rest

O Father God,
why do I push myself so,
even though I'm retired?
Why can't I sit and enjoy
the play of sunlight on the fern
in my front window?
Am I trying to prove something?
Is it the work ethic
prodding me on?
Must I be on the go—
engaged every minute—
to keep from being bored?
Father God, give me the peace
of simple enjoyment.
Let me rest in you
and let go of meaningless activity.

Matthew 11:28-30:
**"Come to me, all you that are weary and are carrying
heavy burdens, and I will give you rest. Take my yoke
upon you, and learn from me; for I am gentle and
humble in heart, and you will find rest for your souls.
For my yoke is easy, and my burden is light."**

How Long?

I lie here, Lord,
unable to move.
People come and go.
They don't know
if I'm really with them or not.
I'm not always sure myself.
Memories mix with the present.
They dress me,
prop me up,
and set me, like a bag of potatoes,
in front of the TV.
Lord, have mercy.
Let me come to you soon.
I want to dance,
see old friends,
and feel good again.
My cry goes up, "How long?"

Romans 8:26:
**Likewise the Spirit helps us in our weakness; for we
do not know how to pray as we ought, but that very
Spirit intercedes with sighs too deep for words.**

Down in the Dumps

O Lord, yesterday
when I realized
that my dream
was not coming true,
I sank down in the dumps,
way down.
So I grabbed my hymnal
and began to sing
"The Church's One Foundation"
and wept.
Then I sang
one hymn after another,
ending with
"Rejoice, the Lord is King."
Thank you, Lord,
for the message of hymns
and for seeing me through.

Matthew 8:24-26:
A windstorm arose on the sea, so great that the boat was being swamped by the waves; but he was asleep. And they went and woke him up, saying, "Lord, save us! We are perishing!" And he said to them, "Why are you afraid, you of little faith?" Then he got up and rebuked the winds and the sea; and there was a dead calm.

Squirrels

Lord of Creation,
when we were small,
our neighbor shot the squirrels
in his pear trees.
We thought
he was a mean old man.
Now I chase the squirrels
who take the stuffing
out of our deck chairs.
Do the children next door
think I'm a mean old woman?
Probably not.
They are too busy
to think of me at all.
Neighbors don't stay home
these days.
Only the squirrels are the same:
ornery as ever,
or are we the ornery ones?
You mentioned sparrows, Lord,
but what about the squirrels?

Genesis 1:25:

God made the wild animals of the earth of every kind, and the cattle of every kind, and everything that creeps upon the ground of every kind. And God saw that it was good.

Matthew 10:29:

"Are not two sparrows sold for a penny? Yet not one of them will fall to the ground apart from your Father."

Unsettled

O Lord, I thought in old age
I would sail off into the sunset,
my life settled.
Now my grandson is in trouble,
and my granddaughter
is having a difficult time.
You know I love them.
My heart is full of sorrow.
I try to understand
how this could happen.
Help me to teach them your way, O Lord,
that they may know the joy
of living in your kingdom.
I rely on your mercy, Lord,
and mercy for future generations.

Psalm 71:18:
So even to old age and gray hairs,
  O God, do not forsake me,
until I proclaim your might
  to all the generations to come.

2 Timothy 2:15:
**Do your best to present yourself to God as one
approved by him, a worker who has no need to be
ashamed, rightly explaining the word of truth.**

Weather Bulletin

It's drizzling, Lord.
The last leaves are floating down.
When I was working,
such weather was an inconvenience;
but now,
it affects my mood
for the day.
Give me a jump-start, Lord.
I need to feel useful.
Is there yet some way
that I can serve?
Give me an assignment
for today.

Ephesians 6:7:
Render service with enthusiasm, as to the Lord and not to men and women.

Romans 12:6:
We have gifts that differ according to the grace given to us: prophecy, in proportion to faith; ministry, in ministering; the teacher, in teaching; the exhorter, in exhortation; the giver, in generosity; the leader, in diligence; the compassionate, in cheerfulness.

Affirmation

O Lord, my God,
what am I to do?
I worked so hard
to achieve my goal.
I prayed.
I thought it was your will.
But it didn't happen.
If I had succeeded, Lord,
I would have felt affirmed.
Help me to accept
what you have for me.
See me through this time.
Help me to put my whole trust
in you.

Psalm 37:4:
Take delight in the LORD,
**   and he will give you the desires of your heart.**

Dead Spaces

Ah, Lord,
There are dead spaces
in my soul:
spaces with dank, moldy air,
which the breath of spring
doesn't reach.
The breeze reminds me
of your creative breath
that soothes,
gives meaning, purpose,
and direction in life.
Breathe on the hollow spaces
of my soul,
O my Lord.
Enliven my life.

Romans 8:11:
If the Spirit of him who raised Jesus from the dead
dwells in you, he who raised Christ from the dead will
give life to your mortal bodies also through his Spirit
that dwells in you.

Suffering

O Lord, my child died today.
That's not supposed to happen.
Children are supposed to
carry on after their parents go.
My heart is sore.
Carry me.
The child you gave me to love
is now yours.
I do not want to be soothed.
The pain is what I have left.
Only assure me of your love,
that I may yet look forward
to joy in the morning.

Psalm 119:28:
My soul melts away for sorrow;
**   strengthen me according to your word.**

CONFESSION

I said, "I will confess my transgressions to the LORD,"
and you forgave the guilt of my sin.

—Psalm 32:5b

Open My Eyes

Sorrow overwhelms,
tears blur my sight.
It's hard to believe
my friend is really dead,
but some things cannot be denied.
Why didn't I visit?
Why didn't I call or write?
Forgive me, Lord.
I missed chances to love
and be loved.
Open my eyes and heart.
Strengthen my resolve,
that I may not miss other opportunities.
Guide me in your way of love.

Isaiah 58:11:
The LORD will guide you continually,
  and satisfy your needs in parched places,
  and make your bones strong.

Hymn: "Open My Eyes, That I May See"

Listening

My mouth is propped open,
stuffed with cotton pads.
The dentist
continues to talk
and asks questions,
which he answers.
I can only grunt.
I wonder if
I have done this to others:
asked questions
and given the answers,
rather than waiting
for a response.
Forgive me, Lord.
Help me to listen
expectantly
to others,
just as we want you
to listen to us.

Psalm 66:19:
But truly God has listened;
he has given heed to the words of my prayer.

Grounded

O Lord, I'm grounded.
They took away my driver's license.
My vision is cloudy,
I don't hear very well,
my reflexes are slow;
but still, it's a blow.
I'm glad they did it
before I had an accident,
but it isn't easy.
Now I am dependent
on others.
O Lord, it's hard to ask for a ride.
Humility is not my style.
Forgive me, Lord.
I need help.

Psalm 51:17:
The sacrifice acceptable to God is a broken spirit;
   a broken and contrite heart, O God, you will not
      despise.

Procrastination

The birds have quieted,
their work day begins:
finding food
and feeding the young.
The dramatic slant
of morning light is lost
as the sun climbs overhead.
The dew dries,
yet I procrastinate.
Then your mosquito
has its way
of moving me on to the
work of the day.
Magnificent God,
is the true measure
of your wondrous creation
in the details?
Is it the fine touch
that inspires?

Psalm 104:24:
O Lord, how manifold are your works!
  In wisdom you have made them all;
  the earth is full of your creatures.

Cranky

Rushing, rushing.
Waiting, waiting.
It is easy to be irritated
when I hurry
or when I wait.
I get cranky
and take it out on others.
Forgive me, Lord.
You promise peace.
Give of your Spirit
to guide and deliver me
that rushing or waiting,
I may be at peace in you.

Colossians 3:15:
And let the peace of Christ rule in your hearts, to which indeed you were called in the one body. And be thankful.

Social Unrest

Every day you give the drama
of the rising sun;
every night, the mystery
of the moon.
Yet we, your people, Lord,
fill the time
with frenzy and frustration.
Ah, Lord, where can we
ascend your holy hill?
Where can we find the peace
that passes understanding?
Save us, Lord.
Put a new and right spirit
within us,
that we may yet
come before your throne
to be clothed with glory.

Psalm 51:10:
Create in me a clean heart, O God,
   and put a new and right spirit within me.

Competition

O Spirit of the Living God,
we sat there
comparing operations,
medical procedures,
and pains,
as though competing
for a prize.
Competition is the habit
of a lifetime
of trying to make ourselves important.
Forgive our foolishness.
Fill us with your Spirit,
that lifts and draws us
together in fellowship.

Galatians 5:25-26:
If we live by the Spirit, let us also be guided by the Spirit. Let us not become conceited, competing against one another, envying one another.

Needy

Lord Jesus, even though
you stand at my right hand,
I think so much about my own
needs and desires
that the wants of others
come in a poor second.
Forgive me, Lord.
You give so much.
Your loving presence
upholds me.
Help me to be sensitive
to the needs and wants
of others.
Then give me strength
to stand beside them
with love.

Hebrews 4:16:
**Let us therefore approach the throne of grace with
boldness, so that we may receive mercy and find
grace to help in time of need.**

Intercession

Sitting through this funeral, Lord,
I can't help wondering
if death is really
a blessing in disguise.
Not because it means
the end of suffering,
but because otherwise
people are not serious
about life.
We do so many
idiotic things.
If death did not wake us up
once in a while,
we would be even crazier.
O Lord, forgive us
for our foolishness.
Guide us in your way
of truth and love.

John 16:13a:
"When the Spirit of truth comes, he will guide you into all the truth."

Hymn: "Dear Lord and Father of Mankind"

Fear of Rejection

Lord of all,
my life has been so circumspect,
so small,
when it could have been
so much larger.
Fear of rejection
has kept me
from so much.
O Lord, show me now
what I can be,
even at this late date.
Give me the confidence,
not to prove myself,
but to be the creation
you intend.

1 John 4:18a:
There is no fear in love, but perfect love casts out fear.

Pride

O Gracious God,
a young couple
stood up and gave
my husband and me
their seats on the subway.
We were grateful,
but had mixed feelings.
Do we look so decrepit?
Thank you, God,
for your care of us
through others;
but I need help
with my pride
along with physical aid.
O God, thank you
for loving us in spite of all
our foolishness.

Proverbs 16:18:
Pride goes before destruction,
   and a haughty spirit before a fall.

Habakkuk 2:4:
Look at the proud!
   Their spirit is not right in them,
   but the righteous live by their faith.

Impatience

You know, Lord,
that I am impatient.
It is so hard for me
to sit still in meetings
while people chatter on and on.
It is hard for me
when my friend
starts in on the past.
Some people call it
life review,
but I am interested
in life now.
Give me patience, Lord.
I need it.

1 Corinthians 13:4a:
Love is patient; love is kind.

Quandary

O Father God,
what am I to do?
I never expected
to outlive my wife.
The odds are against it.
It's not only grieving
over her death,
it's also feeling helpless.
How can I manage?
She gave direction
and meaning to my life.
I guess I have been
shortsighted. Fill me in, God.
Direct me in your everlasting path.
Then I will know
what to do about
the cooking and cleaning.

Psalm 37:5:
Commit your way to the LORD;
trust in him, and he will act.

Your World

O Creator God,
how we misuse
this wonderful world
you created for us.
Our greed
causes us to
poison the water and air,
the fish and plants,
until we, ourselves, are in danger.
Forgive us, O Creator God.
Recreate us
with your Spirit
so that we learn to
care for each other
and for our world.

Romans 8:19, 21a:
For the creation waits with eager longing for the
revealing of the children of God; . . . that the creation
itself will be set free from its bondage to decay.

Picking Up the Pieces

After every storm
I pick up sticks in the yard.
It's good exercise.
In childhood, I always wanted
to clean up the forest.
Now I have an excuse.
I wish cleaning up my life
after a blow-up
were that easy.
You know, Lord, I have a temper.
I hurt others
with words that just fly out.
Forgive me, Merciful God.
I try to make amends to others,
but it still hurts.
I need to change.
Give me wisdom, Lord,
to understand and
overcome this failing.

1 John 1:9:
If we confess our sins, he who is faithful and just will
forgive us our sins and cleanse us from all unright-
eousness.

James 1:5:
If any of you is lacking in wisdom, ask God, who gives to all generously and ungrudgingly, and it will be given you.

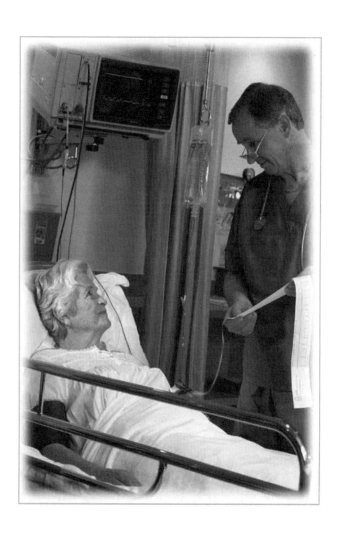

THANK YOU

Praise the LORD!
O give thanks to the LORD, for he is good;
for his steadfast love endures forever.

—*Psalm 106:1*

I Don't Like Secrets

As a child
I kept so many
family secrets.
Now, when people say,
"Don't tell anyone,"
I'm afraid I'll forget
and tell.
I'm so glad
that you know all our secrets, Lord,
and that we can tell you
anything.
It makes life less complicated.
Thank you, Lord,
for loving us as we are.

Psalm 51:6:
You desire truth in the inward being;
therefore teach me wisdom in my secret heart.

Signs

O Lord of love,
a devotion I read
suggested that I look every day
for a sign of your presence in my life.

I tried it this week
and am amazed to see
your acts day by day.
It may be help from a loved one,
flowers blooming,
or someone calling with good news.
When you answer prayer,
I am filled with awe.
Thank you for signs of your presence
here and now.

John 2:11:
Jesus did this [changed water into wine], the first of his signs, in Cana of Galilee, and revealed his glory; and his disciples believed in him.

Aroma Therapy

O Glorious Creator,
spring comes again.
Hyacinths
nearly knock me out
with their scent.
But I don't complain—
they push up,
lush and full of life.
Their glorious
perfume makes me more alert.
Thank you for my nose and
for the reminder
of fuller glory to come.

Song of Solomon 6:2:
My beloved has gone down to his garden,
to the beds of spices,
to pasture his flock in the gardens,
and to gather lilies.

Too Busy

O Lord, I no sooner take on
one job than two arrive.
On top of everything else
I realized that refreshments
were expected at a meeting.
I didn't want to ask
someone else.
Then a dear person
offered to bring a cake.
What a help!
It not only freed me
from the responsibility
but also warmed my heart
that someone thought of it.
Thank you, Lord,
for your many loving servants.

Colossians 3:12:
**As God's chosen ones, holy and beloved, clothe your-
selves with compassion, kindness, humility, meek-
ness, and patience.**

Curiosity

Now we have landed on Mars, Lord.
We are curious about things.
Some think it's wrong
to go this far.
But it opens my eyes
to the vastness
of creation,
gives me a wider vision,
makes me humble.
It gives a hint
of your breathtaking
creative mind.
Thank you, Lord,
that we are part of your creation.

Psalm 8:3-4:
When I look at your heavens, the work of your
**   fingers,**
**   the moon and the stars that you have established;**
what are human beings that you are mindful of them,
**   mortals that you care for them?**

Recipes

Dear Lord,
this morning I looked
through recipes—
marked in cookbooks,
received from friends,
and cut from newspapers.
Some are smudged from use.
They remind me of parties and
happy family gatherings.
There is not time
to try all the recipes I've saved,
but I can't throw any away yet;
it might be just the one I want.
Thank you for the joy
of your presence as we eat
and gather in your name.
We look forward to even greater things.

Matthew 22:2:
**"The kingdom of heaven may be compared to a king
who gave a wedding banquet. . . ."**

John 6:35:
**Jesus said to them, "I am the bread of life. Whoever
comes to me will never be hungry, and whoever
believes in me will never be thirsty."**

Transformation

Morning light awakens me
to a fresh new day.
O God of might and power,
you give sunshine and rain,
flowers and dew,
trees in amazing shapes,
and creatures small and large.
You gave a Son
to show us love
and your very Spirit
to transform us.
I marvel as I see the works of love
your followers perform.
Then my naturally shy, critical nature
becomes more open, generous, and loving.
Thank you, Almighty God.

John 1:16:
From his fullness we have all received, grace upon grace.

Hymn: "How Great Thou Art"

This Is the Day

Dear Lord,
how grateful I am
that my husband and I
have this time together.
He was diagnosed
with one month to live
several months ago.
This is a very special time
of being together
and saying goodbye.
In our nineties, Lord,
we can't waste time on yesterday
or tomorrow. You have given us today.
Thank you for being with us
and giving us cause to rejoice.

Psalm 118:24:
This is the day that the LORD has made;
let us rejoice and be glad in it.

Now Is the Time

Lord, when my visitor asked,
"How are you getting along?"
I hesitated.
My husband is now difficult to rouse
and was in the next room asleep.
Then I said,
"Now is the time of my life.
Our children come every weekend
to be with us.
They take turns.
The nurses and therapists
are thoughtful and caring.
We have a lady who stays every night.
People come by.
It is a time of joy."
My visitor looked surprised.
Lord, I am grateful
that so many care.
Thank you.

Ecclesiastes 11:8a:
Even those who live many years should rejoice in them all.

Gifts

The lacey trees of winter
tell of your handiwork,
O God,
as much as the
tiny buds of spring.
I can walk along a forest path
or water plants in my room,
and you speak to me.
As I gaze at the stars
or watch a sunset unfold
in myriad colors,
my nerves get settled.
With awesome gifts,
You enfold me
in love.
Thank you.

Psalm 19:1-4:
The heavens are telling the glory of God;
   and the firmament proclaims his handiwork.
Day to day pours forth speech,
   and night to night declares knowledge.
There is no speech, nor are there words;
   their voice is not heard;
yet their voice goes out through all the earth,
   and their words to the end of the world.

Dancing

Dear Lord, how I love to dance.
My husband and I danced
at our wedding anniversary.
We jitterbugged
to Big Band music.
Others did too.
It's good exercise,
makes us feel peppy.
Dancing increases our joy
and renews our love.
Thank you, Lord, for joy,
for our love,
and for the fun of dancing.

Ecclesiastes 3:1, 4:
For everything there is a season,
and a time for every matter under heaven . . .
a time to weep, and a time to laugh;
a time to mourn, and a time to dance . . .

Birthday Celebration

Another birthday, Lord.
My friends are taking me
out to lunch.
My family will get together soon
to celebrate.
There will be presents
even though I don't need a thing.
But presents are fun,
even at my age.
It's the mystery before
removing the paper,
and the surprise.
It's nice to be remembered
and fussed over.
Thank you, Lord,
for family and friends.

1 Corinthians 13:13:
And now faith, hope, and love abide, these three; and the greatest of these is love.

Matthew 2:11b:
Then, opening their treasure chests, they offered him gifts of gold, frankincense, and myrrh.

The Breath of Life

The breeze in the garden
or the woods
enlivens me.
Your breath, O God,
gives life within,
purpose, and direction.
When you stir us up,
we are invigorated
and do not lose heart.
Then we go out,
once again,
to do your will in a world
of sorrow.
You fill us with good gifts.
We thank you and praise you
for life in your Spirit.

Psalm 150:6:
Let everything that breathes praise the LORD!
Praise the LORD!

Pets

Thank you, Lord,
for those who
rewrote the rules
to allow pets
in this healthcare center.
All the changes
in coming here
are difficult enough
without having to give up
my dog.
And Rusty would miss
all the little
treats he likes.
Thank you, Lord,
for inspiring your servants
to care.

Psalm 36:5-6:
Your steadfast love, O LORD, extends to the heavens,
   your faithfulness to the clouds.
Your righteousness is like the mighty mountains,
   your judgments are like the great deep;
   you save humans and animals alike, O LORD.

Business in the Night

The spider has been at work
early and late.
A gossamer web
hovers over the houseplants
yesterday transferred to the deck.
The radials glisten
as the breeze shifts,
while the joints of the circling strands
sport tiny glistening drops
from last night's rain.
O Creative God,
thank you for your surprises.
What if we did not notice
your unexpected gifts?
How poor we would be.
Keep our eyes open, O Creator,
for our opportunities to give you thanks.

Psalm 92:4:
For you, O LORD, have made me glad by your work;
  at the works of your hands I sing for joy.

Sight

Thank you, Lord,
that my cataracts are gone.
Thank you for the medical people
who brought this about.
O loving God,
I didn't know
there were so many little birds
in my yard.
And I didn't know my house
was so dusty.
I have to get busy.
The sunshine is so bright.
What a precious gift
is sight.
Thank you, Lord.
Praise! Praise! Praise!

Luke 18:43:
**Immediately he regained his sight and followed him,
glorifying God; and all the people, when they saw it,
praised God.**

Swirling Leaves

Falling leaves remind me
of passing seasons.
I remember raking them up,
jumping in them,
and having bonfires with hot dogs
and marshmallows.
Now my leaves
have to be bundled,
left in the street for the sweeper,
or used in compost.
It's not as much fun.
Now we go to pick
pumpkins or apples
to celebrate fall.
But leaves swirling down
on days of glorious sunshine
are still the same.
Thank you, Glorious God.

Acts 14:17:
Yet he has not left himself without a witness in doing good—giving you rains from heaven and fruitful seasons, and filling you with food and your hearts with joy.

Grandson

O Lord of All,
it's hard to admit
I can't open a pickle jar
or carry my wife's plants
in for the winter.
My grandson brought in the plants.
He helps me keep up the yard.
The other day, he came by
to play catch and used
a lacrosse stick, while
I used my old baseball mitt.
We reach across
the generations.
It is heartwarming
to see him wanting to
keep in touch and help out.
Thank you, God, for the joy
of grandchildren.

Proverbs 17:6a:
Grandchildren are the crown of the aged.

Like a Mother Hen

O God, like a mother hen
you shelter me
under your wing.
I've been under the weather,
and someone from the church
brought me dinner.
Our church has a group
that e-mails one another
to provide meals or rides
for those who need it.
Thank you, God,
for the church
and for your constant care.

Psalm 36:7:
How precious is your steadfast love, O God!
All people may take refuge in the shadow of your
wings.

Looking Forward

O Lord my God,
I look at my hands,
bony and stiff.
My legs are like sticks
and no longer hold me up.
Yet, inside myself,
I feel strong
because you are with me.
Your presence comforts me.
I sit, smiling,
looking out of this body
that no longer works,
and look forward
to indescribable joy.
Thank you, God,
for a lifetime of love.

2 Corinthians 4:17:
For this slight momentary affliction is preparing us
for an eternal weight of glory beyond all measure.

Children's Children

Thank you, dear Lord,
for children.
It warms my heart
to see them grow up,
take responsibility,
adjust to new circumstances,
and carry on family traditions.
Thank you, Lord,
for your unchanging love
passed from generation
to generation.
It is reassuring
that you remain the same.
Thank you for your mercy to us.

Luke 1:50:
**"His mercy is for those who fear him
from generation to generation."**

Hymn: "Great Is Thy Faithfulness"

Mothers and Grandmothers

Dear Lord,
how grateful I am
that my mother and grandmothers
set your path
before me
in early childhood.
With admonitions,
fried chicken,
mashed potatoes and gravy,
and apple pie,
they showed your way by love.
They gave of themselves
so I would see and understand.
Thank you, dear Lord.
Help my grandchildren
see your light.

2 Timothy 1:5:
I am reminded of your sincere faith, a faith that lived first in your grandmother Lois and your mother Eunice and now, I am sure, lives in you.

Psalm 27:1:
The LORD is my light and my salvation.

Church Bazaar

The church bazaar
was held today.
A dear person
gave me a ride
so I could attend.
I felt left out
because I couldn't do
the things I used to do.
Then someone told me,
"Your smile makes everyone
feel welcome."
Thank you, Lord,
for giving me a role
and for those who
tell me I'm needed.

1 Peter 4:8a, 9a:
Above all, maintain constant love for one another. . . .
Be hospitable to one another.

Sparrows

O God of Creation,
sparrows are
wonderful reminders
of your love.
Small and brown,
they crowd around the feed tray,
jostling each other,
chattering,
and picking lice.
That you care
for such heedless creatures
makes me smile.
It gives me hope
that in spite of
our foolish self-absorption,
you love us.
Thank you, God, for caring
for us all.

Luke 12:6, 7b:
**"Are not five sparrows sold for two pennies? Yet not
one of them is forgotten in God's sight. . . . Do not be
afraid; you are of more value than many sparrows."**

Night Watch

O Lord, my God,
When I lie awake at night,
troubles drag me down until
I turn my thoughts to you.
Then I remember your mercies to me,
the joy of sharing your presence
in our congregation,
and the wonders you perform
in the lives of the faithful.
Then my fears subside.
I thank you and praise you
that you are always with us.

Psalm 63:5b-6:
And my mouth praises you with joyful lips
when I think of you on my bed,
and meditate on you in the watches of the night.

Sleep

Thank you, Lord,
for a night of restful sleep.
So often I am awake,
straining and tense
for the coming day,
trying to organize
too many activities.
Then I miss the early time
of quiet with you.
Help me place my anxieties
in your care,
Lord of night and day,
that I may praise you
every morning.

Psalm 92:1-2:
It is good to give thanks to the LORD,
    to sing praises to your name, O Most High;
to declare your steadfast love in the morning,
    and your faithfulness by night.

Singing

The holidays are coming.
I can't shop. I can't wrap;
my fingers tangle
in the string.
My singing isn't the best;
but as I hum,
the words come back to me:
"O Come All Ye Faithful,"
"Silent Night,"
"Joy to the World."
The verses take on meaning
I never noticed before.
How much hymn writers
pack into a few words!
Thank you, Lord, for your
messengers of song.
They bring the message home.

Luke 2:10 (KJV):
And the angel said unto them, Fear not: for, behold,
I bring you good tidings of great joy, which shall be to
all people.

Spring Colors

O Great Father,
as spring comes,
the grass is green,
the sky is blue,
primroses and tulips
are bright and cheery.
Color wakes us
as from a long sleep.
Thank you
for the joy of renewal.
Thank you, Great Father,
for such splendid gifts.

Psalm 107:1:
O give thanks to the LORD, for he is good;
**   for his steadfast love endures forever.**

James 1:17 (KJV):
Every good gift and every perfect gift is from above,
and cometh down from the Father of lights, with
whom is no variableness, neither shadow of turning.

Baldy

Heavenly Father,
the nurses' aide likes
to kid me about my shiny dome.
I remember how sensitive
I was when my bald spot
first appeared.
Now, I'm just glad
for the attention
it gives me
from a young person.
Thank you, Father,
that you value
each one of us
just as we are.

Matthew 10:30-31:
"And even the hairs of your head are all counted. So do not be afraid; you are of more value than many sparrows."

Fruit

When I enter the grocery,
I marvel at colorful fruit
from all over the world:
oranges from Florida,
apples from Oregon,
kiwi from New Zealand,
grapes from Chile.
Thank you, Creative God.
It is amazing
that we can have fresh fruit
at any time of the year.
Thank you, God,
for your delicious gifts.

Genesis 1:11:
Then God said, "Let the earth put forth vegetation:
plants yielding seed, and fruit trees of every kind on
earth that bear fruit with the seed in it." And it was so.

Little Creatures

O Loving God,
the chipmunk dashes by.
Squirrels play
hide and seek around
the tree trunks.
A rabbit pauses
in the garden
to see if I will get up
and shoo him out.
It makes me smile.
What a joy
to sit and watch
little animals
going about their business.
Thank you, God,
for your fascinating creations.

Revelation 5:13:
**Then I heard every creature in heaven and on earth
and under the earth and in the sea, and all that is in
them, singing.**

PRESENCE

While Peter was still speaking, the Holy Spirit fell upon all who heard the word. The circumcised believers who had come with Peter were astounded that the gift of the Holy Spirit had been poured out even on the Gentiles.

—Acts 10:44-45

Church Service

When I was young
and was made to go to church,
I didn't realize
what a gift it was.
Now, when I get my bones together
and have a ride,
I sit in the service
soaking up the joy
of worshiping with others.
I am refreshed
as words are shared
and your Spirit descends upon us.
It sets me up for the week
of my own devotions.
Thank you, Living God,
for your presence among us.

Acts 2:17a:
"In the last days it will be, God declares,
that I will pour out my Spirit upon all flesh."

Keeping Watch

Dear Lord,
as "Silent Night" descends,
there is clattering of carts
in the hall.
Nurses are singing softly,
somewhere.
The night is filled with stars,
candles in churches,
smell of pine.
I think of the hillside in Bethlehem,
with shepherds keeping watch,
as you keep watch with me
on this night of memories.
Your presence is what matters, Lord.
Thank you for being here.

Psalm 23:1:
The LORD is my shepherd, I shall not want.

Psalm 139:9-10:
If I take the wings of the morning
   and settle at the farthest limits of the sea,
even there your hand shall lead me,
   and your right hand shall hold me fast.

Christmas

O beneficent King,
the holidays are coming.
Will anyone invite me for dinner?
Will we have a special meal
in our retirement center?
Will I be able to go to church?
How will I celebrate?
When I remember
the glow of manger scenes,
candlelight services,
and Christmas trees,
I sense your presence
in my heart,
Great and Gracious King,
and I rejoice.

Psalm 16:11b:
In your presence there is fullness of joy.

Guests

Having guests for lunch or dinner
and surprising them
with some new dish
is a joy.
As we bless the food,
we are reminded
of your presence among us.
Sometimes, as we share
the food and our lives,
we sense your Spirit
lifting us beyond ourselves
with unexplained joy
and making us one.
Thank you, Gracious God,
for fellowship
and your living presence.

Matthew 18:20:
**"For where two or three are gathered in my name, I
am there among them."**

Company

Company is coming, Lord.
I didn't think
I could do it anymore;
but everyone is bringing something
so it's easier,
a sort of potluck,
except I know that it's
salad, vegetable, and dessert.
It's church people,
so I'm not nervous.
Bless our gathering, Lord.
Refresh us with your presence
among us.

Luke 24:30-31:
When he was at the table with them, he took bread, blessed and broke it, and gave it to them. Then their eyes were opened, and they recognized him; and he vanished from their sight.

Sharing

Yesterday, Lord,
I visited a friend.
We talked of church activities,
but not about you.
I don't want to be intrusive,
as I was sometimes in youth,
and put people off.
But I would like to share
your presence with others,
the sense of oneness
in your name.
When others do this,
it is so meaningful.
Help me, Lord; show me
what to do.
I shall be looking
to follow your lead.

John 17:21b-22:
**"As you, Father, are in me and I am in you, may they
also be in us, so that the world may believe that you
have sent me. The glory that you have given me I have
given them, so that they may be one, as we are one."**

My Friend

O Lord, my friend is in ICU
I can't visit her.
Surround her with your healing light.
May your Spirit
warm all the particles of her being.
She is not that old.
She has been hurting
a long time.
She needs your presence, Lord,
to inspire.
Relieve her pain.
Heal her with your great love,
that she may live.

Matthew 8:13:
And to the centurion Jesus said, "Go; let it be done
for you according to your faith." And the servant was
healed in that hour.

Take My Hand

Dear Lord, when I see
some of my friends lingering,
diminishing piece by piece,
I sorrow for them
and their families.
I pray
that when my time comes,
it will be quick.
I look forward
to being made whole
and rejoicing in your presence.
I want to be able to sing
and dance
and hear the heavenly music.
Take my hand, Lord;
lead me on.

Revelation 5:11a, 12a:
Then I looked, and I heard the voice of many angels
surrounding the throne and the living creatures and
the elders . . . singing with full voice.

Hymn: "Precious Lord, Take My Hand"

Life

O Great I AM,
around us, within us, among us,
we come before you
to know truth,
to be held in your love,
to be filled with your presence within,
to be given life.
Help me fulfill
your purposes for me
until my last breath
and beyond.
Come, Lord Jesus,
I come to you.

John 14:3:
**"And if I go and prepare a place for you, I will come
again and will take you to myself, so that where I am,
there you may be also."**

God Is

O God of heaven and earth,
as I get older
reality presses in around me.
The hopes and dreams
of youth and middle age
are replaced
by what is.
You who name yourself "I AM"
are more with me than ever.
I learn of you from what is.
As I look back,
I see your hand
determining my path.
Thank you, for being with me
even when I am unaware.

Exodus 3:14:
**God said to Moses, "I AM WHO I AM." He said further,
"Thus you shall say to the Israelites, 'I AM has sent me
to you.'"**

Quiet Time

Now is our time, Lord,
to talk with each other.
I get up early
because I can't sleep.
Yet I do many little chores
before I settle down
for renewal in your presence.
Fill me, O Lord.
The day ahead is busy.
Keep me centered on your love
so that every activity
flows in a life-giving stream.
Then I will be able
to see you in others,
and all will be well.

John 14:21:
**"They who have my commandments and keep them
are those who love me; and those who love me will be
loved by my Father, and I will love them and reveal
myself to them."**

John 15:9:
**"As the Father has loved me, so I have loved you;
abide in my love."**

Need Filling

O Lord, I was so busy
getting things done
that I ran out of gas.
Why, at my age,
do I still
need to be reminded
that I can't run on empty?
You stop me.
Then I remember
that I need to fill up
in your presence
every day to keep going.
Thank you, once again,
for coming to my rescue
by being there.

Psalm 107:9:
For he satisfies the thirsty,
    and the hungry he fills with good things.

Gazing Out the Window

O Lord, when I was a child
I asked my grandma
why she stayed in the house
all the time,
when being outside
was more fun.
She said, "Someday you'll know."
Now, I do.
I look out the window
more often than I go out.
It's not only the weather,
it's feeling safe
in the predictable.
Whether inside or outside,
help me know
that you are always near.

Romans 8:38:
For I am convinced that neither death, nor life, nor angels, nor rulers, nor things present, nor things to come, nor powers, nor height, nor depth, nor anything else in all creation, will be able to separate us from the love of God in Christ Jesus our Lord.

Recognition

Sitting early in the garden, O Lord,
I am reminded
of Mary Magdalene,
who recognized you
in the face of a gardener.
In Emmaus,
in the breaking of bread (Luke 24:30-31),
the disciples
saw you in the face
of a stranger.
O Lord, remind me
to look for you
in the faces of others.
Your presence among us
sustains us.

John 20:15:
Jesus said to her, "Woman, why are you weeping? Whom are you looking for?" Supposing him to be the gardener, she said to him, "Sir, if you have carried him away, tell me where you have laid him, and I will take him away."

Hymn: "In the Garden (I Come to the Garden Alone)"

Hugs Needed

O Lord Jesus,
I live alone.
No one has touched me for days,
let alone hugged me.
How I long for enfolding arms.
As a child, after my mother died,
I remember watching
other children
embraced by their mothers
and feeling the ache inside.
Now it's that way again.
I've read that we need a hug
every day.
I'll vouch for that.
O Lord, I need your presence
in human form.

Mark 10:13a, 16:
People were bringing little children to him in order
that he might touch them . . . And he took them up in
his arms, laid his hands on them, and blessed them.

Hymn: "The Sweet Story of Old"

Mourning

"Time to go on—"
that's what she said to me
this morning.
Cruel truth.
O Lord, I am not ready.
Comfort me, in my fog, merciful God.
Even Job's comforters
sat with him for seven days and seven nights
before they began
to rationalize his suffering.
Sometimes the silence of being there
is what is needed.
Eventually I will move on,
but not yet.
O Lord, thank you for listening
and being with me.

Job 2:13b:
**They sat with him on the ground seven days and seven
nights, and no one spoke a word to him, for they saw
that his suffering was very great.**

Matthew 5:4:
**"Blessed are those who mourn, for they will be com-
forted."**

Circle Meeting

Lord, as our church circle
comes together to
study new ideas
and recall former times,
we celebrate your presence.
Keep us faithful
though our legs shake,
our arms stiffen,
and few can drive.

You call one after the other
to join you on the other side.
We praise you for friends
on both sides of the river.
We are never alone,
for you are with us.

Matthew 28:20b:
"And remember, I am with you always, to the end of the age."

Hymn: "Shall We Gather at the River"

Easter

O Lord, Easter is a time of joy.
I remember
finding Easter eggs,
buying new spring dresses
and Easter bonnets.
People don't fuss
so much anymore.
They wear casual clothes
no matter what the occasion.
I am glad they come
to church
to share the rousing alleluia hymns
no matter what they wear.
Thank you, Lord,
for bestowing new life
by your presence among us.

1 John 4:13:
By this we know that we abide in him and he in us, because he has given us of his Spirit.

Scriptures Cited..........

Hymns Cited..........

ABIDE WITH ME